THE UNDERCARDS

BY
JAMES JAY

GORSKY PRESS
LOS ANGELES • CALIFORNIA
2003

THE UNDERCARDS

copyright © James Jay, 2003

Cover Artwork by Kiyoshi Nakazawa
Cover design by Sean Carswell
second printing, April, 2005

ISBN 0-9668185-5-5

Gorsky Press
PO Box 42024
Los Angeles, CA 90042

TABLE OF CONTENTS

ACKNOWLEDGEMENTS

I wish to express my grateful acknowledgment to the following publications in which some of these poems appeared: *Crab Creek Review* (And So the War Began, Andre Continues Undefeated Streak at the Amboy Sports Arena); *Cutbank* (All of Its Weight); *Flare* (Out of the Smokehouse Bar); *ISLE* (A Refrain on the Colorado Plateau, Camphorweed, Tarantula Dreams); Mississippi Review Online (Pro-Wrestler Andre the Giant Haiku); *Thin Air* (At Tucker Plastics Factory, Ground); *Moon Reader* (Someone Must Have Quit).

Thank you to Mark Gibbons, Ed Lahey, and Miles Waggener for their continual feedback, inspiration, and encouragement on this book. Also thank you to the Arizona Commission on the Arts for grants that allowed time to travel and research and the Baker Writer in Residence program for time and space in which to write.

BARTERING A POEM

for Lola Mae Fulmer

Out of Chloride, out of Oatman, the miners blow in —
Out of the Cerbats, they shuffle forward
into the Café where Lola, my grandmother, works.

Busted, they offer turquoise for coffee,
a silver necklace for eggs and toast,
copper earrings as a tip —

That was the Fifties, that was Kingman.
By the time I arrive on the scene, the Oak Ridge Boys sing
from the jukebox and I get pancakes for weekly chores.

Roads are paved, although sidewalks are still for cities.
I toss Nerf footballs until the goatheads
of every dropped pass pick them to foam — the Seventies.

Now, now I've been wanting to write about my grandmother,
about how when she died we found her box of bartered jewelry,
about how I took a necklace with me.

Like the sad boots of those miners roaming
the high desert, I'm more pieces than plans.
I wish to speak a language of dirt

where what was chiseled, hauled,
and downright blown up sticks to whatever
you wear, to your flesh, to your hair,

and you walk wherever you will
covered in the armor of that busted up syntax.
An intelligent, strong-willed woman looks over the mess.

She will put coffee in front of you,
you will say something like
                    "I am James Jay, don't you remember me?
        I don't need to work retail anymore now that I'm here.
        Today I quit my job! And I too hate taxes. Look at my shirt.
                Don't you see?"

The woman will look, will look again, and say
                                        "Boy,
        handsome boy, you are right. Writing poems
        is more important than paying taxes,
        at least until they arrest you.
                    So, what's that you got on your wrist?"

THE MAYOR

SNAGGED

A tall Hualapai Indian man, big as two men, heaves a basketball sized stone
into the caboose of a permanently parked train.

The metal thuds hollow like a distant shotgun fired
into the park's Andy Devine Days dedication.

The stone crashes to the sidewalk and rolls into the broken mouth of history.
A man wearing a bolo tie taps on the shoulder of another man.

The crowd of picnic people turns to face the caboose.
They are blank, useless, dolls displayed in a hutch.

In tight-hipped steps, clicking heel toe into the scene, the bolo tie man
        and his pal charge.
The Hualapai stoops about for anything solid enough to heave.

With stiff arm topped by fist, the bolo tie man chops down first from behind.
Several more men, younger, in their twenties, trot past folding chairs
        and table cloths.

They throw tentative, picky punches at the pile, winding up,
choosing their shots like baseball pitches.

His hands squeezing the hot metal rail
of the caboose's bannered stairway, a boy watches and wishes for

Andy Devine: the nicest man imaginable, the smiling butt of the jokes, Old Jingles.
Andy Devine: the only celebrity of Kingman, Arizona's Route 66 glory days.

Andy Devine: the swell sidekick of the black and white Westerns. He wishes
Andy Devine would work a fat cheek spell over breaking knuckles

and cracking ribs, a spell that lifts the bleeding bodies
to their feet, a spell that wipes dirt from jeans and makes hands

shake out mistakes, returning men to barbecues and small talk.
What do you make of those holes in history loaded with your silence?

Andy Devine: a spell snagged in tumbleweeds,
tumbleweeds that wait for a high desert wind to blow.

Yards away from failing, and ever failing hands, they holler and a face springs
from arms, shirts, jeans at pavement level — history, pockmarked and scarred

from its chin to its flying black hair; scars run over
its nose and left cheek mainly; its mouth open wide, but no noise comes out;

hard shut lids hide its eyes. History beaten
and broken while men pile on punching and shoving each other's backs, punching

and shoving themselves into pieces of stories, beating themselves
simple, until out of the top the bolo tie man springs —

his hair swept high, his right hand red as dirt beyond the park grass, and he hollers
"He aint no Andy Devine. Not this one. He aint no Andy Devine."

THE MAYOR OF KINGMAN

His skin is like loose leather
or an oversized raincoat.
Shirtless, he walks it around in the sun
along the drifting dirt roads.

Children scuttle behind worn trailers
or flee for the cover of boulders in the wash.
They run up monster stories from the sand
and float them one on top of the next.

In waves, the heat climbs
from the only blacktop road around.
The sun bakes the tires on the roofs
finger press soft.

The mountain to the west looks
like a great feathered chief asleep on his back,
but beneath the brown, cracked rocks of the eyes
there are only cracked rocks.

A stray boy fashions the man,
into a lost grandfather who walks
to him with a secret
he almost forgot to give,

or a wooden ship
pushing through endless blue, a ship he's seen
only in books, a ship now cursed into the skin
of this man who presses on in dirt.

REMAINS OF A COPPER MINE

A dull reflection of red, the side of the mountain
that Duvall Mining claimed wears a jagged space,
drawing up images of the spot on Jupiter,
like a place about to be named after a god,
then blankly abandoned.

The Industrial Park on a flat run
of desert to the east has stolen its name,
forgotten its god, borrowed a god, and become
fragments, fragments of associates that wear shifting
names like Tucker Housewares, Bayline, Ace, Home Co,
names that crawl across warehouses and truck trailers.

On Highway 66, men and women file over
to do the work of boats, plastics, barrels, glass.
The pennies in their pockets show only faint traces
of copper, and even the old timers stammering
out of their Fords are hard pressed
to tell you how they got here.

A BOY'S KNUCKLES SWOLLEN

"I never started a fight with anyone, except bullies. I looked for them, even when I was just a kid, and they'd whip me good. I just couldn't resist them. My busted, little hands were insatiable."

— Jack Hutchinson,
Professional Wrestler

A boy's knuckles swollen like bellies at a buffet
like a crow's feathers at below zero
like a barrel cactus in a monsoon
like rocks in a river, hard and confused,
like the tales told on the bank of an arroyo about the fat kid who breaks the
        backs of cats with 2 x 4s
like water behind a child's daylong piling of rocks
like Truth driving to confession
like Hate answering questions during a first date
like Cruelty conducting a staff meeting
like memory pinned to a third stage Alzheimer patient's gray haired head
like sheetrock left outside all season
like Crusaders rotting on the side of the road to Constantinople
like books in a dumpster
like a newspaper in a puddle on the porch
like a swarm of ants fighting a stirring stick
like bentonite under the wavy roads on the Res
like mistletoe feeding on mesquite
like cumulus clouds over the Black Mountains in July
like a Gila Monster jawing its way through blind rabbits in a warren
like the leather of combat boots crossing contested ground
like your lover's wrists in policeman's handcuffs

FIELD TRIP

A dozen junior high kids watching
ping pong balls in a plastic cage fall:
a lesson in probability, although
all I could think of were ant farms.

Then one broke loose, a brown hair girl,
Lisa may have been her name, landed
by me for a quick hit on the lips.
It was like a first date, I mean very first,

right there in front of everyone. I'd never
even done that kissing in the closet game.
Los Angeles Science Museum, great arching
ceiling and physics strutting its stuff

at every turn, her pretty brown hair
and wide mouthed smile, pretty even if,
back then, Shyness crowed for high standards:
the old Cheryl-Ladd-or-No-One-Ultimatum.

The World, of course, dropped "no one" balls,
one plinking after the next, too damn smart
for me to figure
where they plop.

EVEN AT MIDNIGHT IT'S 100 DEGREES

She believes in Gila Monster Angels that clamp
their jaws so tightly to love
you'd have to cut their heads off
to make them leave.

She calls Russian Thistle Russian Thistle.
The desert at midnight. Its wings mottled
orange and black:
sluggish skin, a slow
glisten, a pause of light
on each bump of flesh.

The swing shift ends, meaning
that between the iron door
of the warehouse and the asphalt
parking lot she stops in the dirt.

The night clear.
The moon full:
            a sun
            warming the wind.

The moon blows light over
her outstretched hands to her sides.
The moon watches her hands
roll their thumbs
across their index fingers,
and it fills her chest with air in a long, drawn inhalation.

She exhales as if to weep,
but merely continuing to drip sweat
walks to her car,
dented and leaking oil.

Nestled in dirt and tumbleweeds
Gila Monster Angels fill the desert
with the washed reflection of reflected light,
and she is the woman I dream that I am

as I stare daily into machines,
machines black-red and swollen, itching
from the smell of clumped grease
and the metallic longing for fire that yields ash.

TWO WIN ON THE NIGHT JANITOR

In the dull light of moon through glass
the kid half steps on his toes
stirring dust from the office carpet,
leading with a jab, then another, then the right
knocking the dickens out of the air,
then back to the broom, then back
to the air, a tangle of cleaning
and some solid shadow boxing that whacks
the night away until the suits arrive early
with the sun, and his head down he slides
the last of his cart and supplies into a closet,
a faint drip of sweat on brow threatening
to rat him out, if someone were to look,
but no one is to look or ever look
as he rides down to the street to deal
with the pavement of the day,
his title an office suite high, plopped
in a plastic bucket that hangs
on the curved crescent of the moon.

SMITE

Later I learned she hooked up
with Jimmy West
and would date him for months,
but on that night I find
myself in Phoenix visiting
a high school, now college, pal
in a people packed
single wide trailer adrift.

Somehow I get lost
in one of those tiny bedrooms
and sit on a bed
with Laura Smite, a crush
since 7th grade. Some Billy Idol tunes heat
the press board walls, the closet door off
its sliding track, someone's dirty clothes there
and here, her hand makes for
my knee, a fantasy of how it would be,
and so I bolt for more beer, for hot summer air,
for the blacktop road.

I just plain freak,
and I write poems about politics ever since —

AT TUCKER PLASTICS FACTORY

Go see Ireno Castaneda. He's your boss for today, but he'll still call you
    the little *jefe*.
So go see Ireno Castaneda because that's better than working in regrind and the
    itchy heat of wrestling defective trash cans, hangars, baskets, and
    crates into the chomping end of a machine.
Go see Ireno because that's better than top-loading barrels or walking
    the rotting boxes in warehouse 3.
Go see Ireno Castaneda. He's the one with the maroon shirt that reads
    "Parump."
Go see Ireno. He's the one with the forearms that are nearly as wide as they are long.
    He'll tip you off. Warn you not to drink ice cold water. Show you
    how to whack nails (not your house nails, but the heavy-ass duty kind)
    into truck trailer floors, secure molds, crank banding wire. And he
    knows money to boot. He'll slip you in on the number 52; 52 being
    the number of hours after which you lose money for OT work - *taxes*
    and all.
So see Ireno. You're clocked in. The sweats already rolling off your tired skin.
Go see Ireno. He'll shove a shoulder between you and the blistering metal
    of a slipping mold.
Go see Ireno Castaneda. At lunch he'll show you wallet pictures of his
    six daughters, and say, smiling, cheeks thick as muscled arms,
    the oldest one is at college in Tucson.
Go see Ireno Castaneda. He's the one who doesn't speak in a dozen 721s, off-
    load 38s, high and tight 46s, or 702s. Instead, he'll sing a tune that's
    not in any English you know, but not in any Spanish you know either.
Go see Ireno Castaneda. He'll sing you a tune like this:
    lo dee da dee da dee da momo momo,
    la dee da dee da dee da mó mó mó mó mó mó.

TARANTULA DREAMS

I scuff my boots through dry, red mud and ask
the man in low orbit over the Mogollon Rim,
"What's scrub oak?" And the man in low orbit
replies, "It'll take seven to ten days to get your message.
You see I'm in low orbit. Sometimes it's longer,
then I must be in high orbit." From the rim
I reply "ah, hah, ah" when Dostoevsky
would have said "what... what... what" or Kerouac
"who ... skoo di dee skoo di doo di dee doo ... who."
So from low orbit the man says to wait, so I do
from down here on a rutted road of brown that meanders
over the rim and into the space of the high desert
below. "But what's scrub oak?" I ask the man
in low orbit again, but not loud enough to stretch
it out to him, and I crack dry twigs and flame
them up for a little extra heat in the early Spring.
The ponderosas root it out in the dry ground.
The cliffs jostle their way into space.
The man in low orbit will speak, but now
I'm sitting flat in front of the fire and wrestling with night
bugs and sounds of birds too hurried to grapple. I wait
and from low orbit hear, "You're scrub oak,"
and from the ground up bones in dead dirt I know.

GROUND

Four ravens rustle about on the nearest roof.
Four ravens begin to pull you from a slouch.

You start the morning hunched on a concrete bench,
your work boots duct taped, the dew from the grass spreading

over the beat silver wrap, your stare rising from the tape,
rising across the thick, round shoulder of the man to your right.

Four ravens, talons clicking on the tin rain gutter, draw you.

The man goes by the name loader, lumper, grounds worker, de la Garza.
His shoulders keep records in muscle.

Each busted job, busted love, flat broke day piled upon the next,
thickening, slowing and waiting to start work. *And you?*

On the bench, you wait for other workers. Some slouched,
some limped, some chest jutted out the way men who know

they're going nowhere walk. Your stare rises over the eaves,
the shingles peeling their way off the roof

as if there were a soul in the sun
trying to give you one more thing to fix.

You settle back to black feathers
playing as blue at dawn. *And the ravens?*

The ravens, talons to rain gutters,
promise more to you than the sun.

BEDINGFIELD

ALL OF ITS WEIGHT

He sees the thin scabs,
        fresh over his right knuckles,
                the blood beneath pressed
back by grease
        and thin, dry hope.

The tips of his fingers
        callused smooth,

he runs them
        across her thigh
                and wishes them

more gentle than they are
or he is
        or thinks he is,

wishes to press
        the full weight of his heart.

(Almost blushes in the dark by thinking of his heart at this time, but he does
        think of his heart,
                then does again.)

And he wishes to press the full weight of his heart
        into his hands,
as if they were things
        apart from himself,
things that can hold
        love as certain
                as a crescent wrench.

But can he wish any more
        into his hands
                already full

of decades
        of work, of fights, of machines?
Which is to say they're already full
        of love,

because his decades
of work, of fights, of machines
are love too,
love that is without words,
love that denies over and over
in grunts and bruises until it forgets
where it belongs or why.

But those things are pushing him
now
into more than they are,

making more for him to wish
into his hands,
gently, gently
coaxing under
the hard pressure
of the mind to move
the heart
into the hands.

And she with the moon's light
cutting through
the bent slats of the window
glides her hands across
his cheek —
his hope fresh,
crisp, sharp.

His hands swallowing
more than ever.

PRO-WRESTLER ANDRE THE GIANT HAIKU

Andre steps over
the ring ropes into the square –
the ground gives a sigh.

        Andre the Giant
        body slams Bruiser — a towel
        drops from the rafters.

    Wrestling boots unlaced —
    Andre runs a blow dryer
    through his hair — real clean.

        Andre's skivvies flap
        on the line — a sunny day.
        A raven doesn't care.

With pen in fingers
Andre writes the universe —
fingers size of hands.

    Andre helps a little
    old lady across heavy
    traffic — the road yields.

        Andre bends far down
        to palm water from the stream.
        The stream stretches up!

Andre wraps his hands
around his foot — massages.
The cheering fans gone.

        Bruiser shoves the clerk
        at the hotel. Vulgar… Watch
        out! Here comes Andre.

Andre snaps fortune
cookies and reads. The chef takes
the rest the day off.

The ground is lonely.
It needs convincing to hold
down rocks. Where's Andre?

Andre skips. BLAM! BLAM!
of heels until the sun shines.
The children go play —

Hard pin! Andre breaks
two ribs, they're Bruiser's —
even giants need money.

A mugger threatens
Andre at knife point. Andre hands
him an autograph.

Andre rides the bus
two seats at a time — snoozing
to the next match up.

Abrakadabra!
But Andre's still big — lonely
curse… fallen brow.

Andre wades into
the sea. The waves carry him
like driftwood — free feet!

DESOLATION LAUGHLIN

I.   Noting

The keno man passes good
luck back with the square paper —
the sheet a copy of blue
crayon and orange ink, faded.

It might mean something, but not
win. It's tossed, blank side up, next
to the empty breakfast plates
on the bar. A girl, a hitch

in her step, left leg fused taught,
sets on top the plates the bill,
so scrawled and thin it can't be
taken seriously to pay.

A dog trots through the open
door. He can't write so he has
no note. He's a dog. He just
trots on through — very simple.

There's a guy named The Cooler,
mustache thick as the dog's hair.
He notes on butcher paper:
great long scrolls wound on metal.

Although he has all the notes,
The Cooler doesn't count up
any better than the rest,
except the dog.   He's (just) a dog.

II.   The Cooler

There's a man called The Cooler.
He's already broken one
arm today, an arm on a boy who
beat him with a cue.

In the confused closing light
of bare bulbs rubbing shadows
on booths and bar The Cooler counted
3 and shoved the boys

towards the door, but there were 4
and the 4th smashed a busted
cue off his neck and shoulder before
he turned to business.

The Cooler, mustache dog hair
dense, rubs his index finger
across his matted lip as he counts
the gaming, drinks, food

on a long sheet of paper.
Everywhere the count's far off:
someone mis-ringing the register,
slipping drinks, shoving

money into their pockets.
Through the hole in the backroom
door, a waitress passes him a cup
of coffee, lukewarm.

At seven in the morning
The Cooler awakes with sweat
on his brow and thick in his coarse hair;
he forgot to thank
the waitress. Very silly
he thinks, grins the thought away.
He rolls to his side, wrapped in blankets,
folds his flat pillow.

29

The light opening slowly
across the carpet, his eyes
gaze at the far wall; his neck sore, taught,
a burden to sleep —

HE WENT OFF AND GOT A REAL JOB
for Steve Kowit

If I ever see Jimbo again, it will be
boxing: Holyfield versus that other guy.
Jimbo's fists filled with cash and a cup of Coors —
all bets on! Or Zazen on phone books taped and piled
high enough to count breaths. Hold all phone calls!
Or chili dogs, on sale, gobbled up all at once.
Memory, name your price.

I WANT TO BE A PROFESSIONAL WRESTLER

And he's not the giant I had hoped for,
this wrestler now flexing and pointing as he crawls
through the ring ropes. Andre the Giant
canceled the announcer said; Andre was sick,
Andre phoned it in, the giant I had hung my hopes on
phoned it in. And I can't imagine Andre as being
sick; he's much too big to be sick. But the announcer
said that he is and tonight we get a small giant,
one barely taller than I am, and I'm not tall,
not tall enough to be a wrestler or else
I would be a wrestler, and I wouldn't be
sick either. And if enough giants fell
ill, then maybe, even at five foot ten, I could wing it,
put on a few pounds, eat corn dogs before bed.
I could call myself the little giant, the constant
giant, the giant who eats his vitamins, chews
apples, gets vaccinated, gets flu shots, and I won't
disappoint. I won't leave you with boiled hamburgers
and warm coca cola in a plastic cup. In this arena
full of bellowing fans, I won't leave you
with nothing to do but think of work, the meeting
you forgot to schedule. I won't be a runt
under the spotlight, a poor show or a no show,
leaving you to dwell on your bathroom's lousy shower
fixtures, your cat shitting on the carpet, your calls
for love limited to faded pleas on an answering machine.
You could ignore the plastic stadium seats
that you can barely shoulder into, even though
you're not a giant, not even close to one,
barely big enough to be a midget. And if enough
giants fell ill, then I'd be the little giant, the constant
giant, and you'd rise from your plastic seat
and up to your toes, lifting your eyes over the fans
in front of you, over their waving signs of cheer,
and you'd be able to see me striding into the ring
with all my sincerity torqued into a Figure Four leg lock.

CORRESPONDENCE

The night breeze filters
    through the window's screen.
The skin of my arm
    assembles the breeze
as memories of my younger brother now
    so foreign to me.

His letter to me is again inside
    its opened envelope on the floor.
He writes that he has a new job
    working for Orange County.
He writes that his Kung Fu practice goes well.
I don't know why I tell you this.
He writes that he likes the poems I sent him a few months ago.
    He asked for them.
He writes once or twice a year —
    one down.
Of course he writes that he liked the poems —
    sincerity?
He writes in printed letters, all caps.
He closes "Look forward to seeing you soon."
He closes "Love."
He closes by printing his name.
Exactly the same close
of the last ten years' letters.

I stare out the window.
The yellow lamp light of the neighbor's
    has deer in it.
It's not unusual, still I watch.
I'll watch them go up the street
    as far as the window allows.
Windows are so loaded.
I hate the word trope.   It means so little.

I want words to work my way to him.
Our relationship is a callused knuckle.
A trope is a scab. Pick it back to blood.

Correspondence

My eyes watch the step, step, pause of the deer —
    the exaggerated hold of their shadow
        on the grass.
The skin of my arm assembles the breeze
    as my brother,
        and my mind is filled with skin.
My eyes are an aside.
I love my brother. I haven't held him in years.
Our embraces are clumsy chests,
    stiff arms to the back.
I thought poems could soften this;
I think he did too.
I don't want to prove anything.
I want another go at it,
    then another one.

I turn my head;
the last of the white tails
    shake out of the yellow light,
out of the shape
    of the window's frame.

I want to make the breeze
    that breaks across the dirty smell
        of the window's screen
into an even pass of air,
air that arrives sitting
on a couch next to itself
leisurely sunk against its weight
letting touch haphazardly speak —

BEDINGFIELD

The bent frame of an ancient man
leans into the boxcar wall

a few feet from the poker game
on the floor and an eye flip

over a boy's shoulder. Old hobos
and new Depression made bums circle

the cards and money in a world
of practically no money.

Eyes drooped in a dull grey,
the ancient man darts his eyes

over the thin, young shoulder.
He lets a sigh pass his nose,

slightly. The boy folds.
A new hand — dart of eyes.

The man stares out the door, keeps silent for stay;
the sound of nothing gives

the boy confidence to take
another card. The man continues his stare

as if recalling a vibrant youth, the cliché
the men at the table expect. Some know

the story of the moonshine that killed
a whole bar, except for this husk,

that they pass off as used,
bent, leaning, the man

whose bones simply fused to pain
overnight. The ancient man could care

less about his bones, the past.
He counts cards. Plays forlorn.

A few days later the man and the boy
meet and split the money, run

the routine in chance encounters
on the same worked route

of railroad towns that cling like weeds
to the line through the Southwest.

The boy is JW, which doesn't stand
for anything, except JW.

                        Except for four years
when JW, drafted by the U.S. Army for WWII,

is dubbed John Walker — the Army not taking any crap
about initials for names.

The Battle of the Bulge... John Walker survives and lasts
four years until honorably discharged.

JW at ninety years old (I'm now the boy
at Bedingfield family reunions),

JW is my great uncle Dub, my grandma Lola's brother,
a reclaiming of name by sounds, Dub. His Texas

accent strong in his gentle voice he speaks
to me on a metal picnic table

under a rusted awning
in the Haulapai Mountains, a park

coincidentally made by the CCC
and I posture my body like his,

my small shoulders rolled forward,
elbows rested on knees, fingers

interlocked and bobbing a bit,
mulling his words in my head

as voices of family run circles
in the mountain air. I imagine

nothing works on coincidence then,
and I glimpse his thin frame,

let my left shoulder sink a little
farther, hold the posture and listen —

STORAGE & TRANSFER

Off to Ovando to uncrate,
        to unpack, to assemble
a table that seats a dozen
        dot com millionaires
or
up Petty Creek with a dozen
        Persian Rugs to unroll:
insured for 1.7 million
        and bouncing in back of an exhaust
                leaking Pack Van.
or
any other cherry run:
        lots of drive time with
limited lumping,
        it all turns out to be a break
                for the back.

Cherry runs: a day unglazed
        by so much sweat and dog fur;
no middleclass sofas and hide-a-beds,
        no torn and worn OS furniture,
        1.5s
        3 cubes
        wardrobes
        dish packs
the hours of packing and loading,
        converting a lifestyle into 18K
of freight, an inventory of
        S.O.s
        Ws
        7s
        12s:
the condition of the crap they got,
        a Dr. Seuss like language speaking their status,
                their place, their worth.

Still, I have to tell you, cherry run or not,
        today when the grandfather clock arrives
on the dock and I unscrew
        the crate revealing the seven foot beast

to be checked, to be signed off,
   to be passed along.

Still, I can't help but want
   to power screw
"Jimbo Hates You"
     right into its face:
12 numbers and confused hands
   wearing my brand!
A cherry run, still, I want to screw its insurance policy
   into its pendulum slot.

What cowardice, what courage,
   what compassion keeps me at bay?
What sends me after the nearby OSHA manual instead,
   sends screws five ways through it,
makes me pitch the manual
   on the break room table
for all to see my work, my art,
     my possibility?
There it rests serving notice
   I'm leaving for the day,
showing I'll be back
     on time tomorrow
because
tonight, after a fistful of beers,
   Jimbo won't really hate millionaires,
they have mothers too, even dot com ones must.
   And when I'm yes ma'amming and
     yes sirring in my clean work shirt,
I'll be thinking inside my thick skull
   about what holds my callused hands,
puts them to work on something else common.
   What is it that Jimbo hates?
Instinct?
or
   maybe he just doesn't know
   when to carve or when to crate
or when to fight or to flee
or when to flee like hell.

MY SWEET, SWEET TRAIN WRECK

A snarl, a squint of blue eyes, grumpily she sits
up after three or four konks on the snooze button.
Red hair rips back with a wild arching hand.

I'm across the room at the computer typing my little poems.
Flogging Molly's whisper from the machine's music player:
"If I should ever leave this world alive."

She hurtles back the blankets, launches
her small, naked body toward the bathroom door.
Wood on wooden frame, the door crams shut behind her.

Like the grey roots of plants seeking something unseen,
the morning light works across my desk, my arms, the walls.
A few minutes, then she's back in the room.

She cat stretches straight up to the stars!
Through a stray eye, she glances at the clock,
then dives under the mess of blankets,

a wave of Pendelton cresting over her head,
and she is gone! My Love has no fear
of time. Dear god, I'd love to be so bold.

To my poems I return and work back into the light
clicking of the keyboard. The Flogging Molly's and I
in our own world of time where light moves
        like a plain old particle.
               Still, we think of waves sometimes.

POETS ARE FOOLS OR WRITER'S BLOCK

February, a break from the cold,
sun and sixty degrees. A fluke!
I get up, open the blinds,
late in the morning and she
says, "lets have sex
          all day." Sunlight fresh
on her pale white profile and shoulder
slipped out of the blankets.
She's Bukowski's distressed goddess.
She's Tyler Durden's mad Marla.
She's older than me by a bit
and has the best body I've ever imagined
on any woman. She knows
she's not what she used to be;
ten years ago I couldn't have touched her.
Now she's down to my level:
artist who hasn't and won't make it.
Down, but still in love
with the smell of tulips and tiger lilies,
with the crawl of sunlight over shacks on the hill,
Ten years ago I wouldn't have had
a shot with something so gorgeous.
Now I pass on her offer, tell her
I have poems to work on,
in particular, "_____
_____" the best line
a fool, a poet fool, ever wrote,
or so I think in February,
a break from the cold,
sun and sixty degrees.

Leaving me to my bad lines,
I send her with coffee mug hanging off her hand
out the door
into the day I wish
I would have made mine, ours, yours.

SAILING

A becalmed summer day, father
       and son bathed in the patience
of irons. The main sail up
       to nothing. The jib a flat smirk.

The father, the skin of his forehead wrinkled
       awaiting a solution, holds
a line in each large fist. The sun
       bounces off the sea, a moot wave.

It can go on like this for hours,
       for days, for years.

Oil islands starboard stern, sea
       lions port bow, the life

vested boy waits too. His palms on the blue
       deck, the smell of salt
the only song they all know.
       The pulse of a body, a tsunami:

a secret they can't speak to each other,
       although both know a bit about tides and stars,
both are willing to learn,
       and both will finally drift alone all night.

CURRENCY

OUT OF THE SMOKEHOUSE BAR

On a 70s Harley he fires
onto the road in a wide sweep, weaves,

slides back into the dirt
in front of me. I work

my car's wheel and brakes to miss the whirl
in the dust and hurtle to a halt

in a tumbleweed wall
splintered and pitched wild

by the hood. I'm out the door; instinct
pushing into the smell of oil, dust

blurred pungent to my nose
and hanging visible

in the moonlight. The biker and bike
on their sides, almost at rest, stuck

to the earth by surprise, stupor.
A voice, muffled, mutters

"my fucking leg" and "help"
slurred by either the biker or me,

When I grip the bent bike handles
to lift the machine from his leg, I slip

in the blood from his head
and baffled by the bike's weight.

My chest, face, arms bloody and black
as his, but whose voice is wrecked mute, dark

and sorry for itself,
its self that dully left

its body in fumes? I spot my hands
and lift them to my forehead,

then lightly move the fingers
down, feel the nose smashed three

fingers to the right, lower the lips
swollen and split foreign to the skin

of the fingers probing
for certainty, probing

for a voice in the mouth that confirms
the possibility of breath, my breath,

my claim of life on life.
A touch to the tongue lifts

the fingers back to self on the thick
taste of iron, and his face flickers

in degrees of red, black:
a death now his to retake.

I kneel in the repose of pain and claim
both voices, his and mine. I remain.

AN ELEGY FOR THE LIVING

The sun-beaten, wooden table on the side of the house wreaks of dirt.
I pull on a bottle of wine slowly and watch the dust from the road fly
on by from the passing of trucks, rusted, busted, and stammering along.

I have come here alone to look after my pal's dog,
to watch over the house, to let the sun beat the wooden table, and to smell
the dust of midsummer whipped up by random waves of broken up vehicles.

In this country of plenty, for the most part, I comply to do my end: my paper-
work, file registrations, get licenses to drive and to fish, cheer at sporting events,
see television movies, read newspapers, wear a watch, return calls…

I lack nothing but guilt, so I pull on a bottle of wine and like a landlocked sailor
or a no port country that waits for a ship to show, a destiny to set in, a something
             to float by
and up the ante for a while, I wait — I muscle around time.

The dog slopes over the porch. His eyes stare at the road and his expression looks
like a wolf's, although I've only seen wolves on televisions and movies. I
             down the last
of the wine, mark time, and we both watch the dirt on the road fly and settle
             as rusted, busted,
trucks stumble by in certain jerks and sudden tugs, ripping by the stop sign
             that's brown
from age and dull by lack of use.

I whisper something that I don't remember (because this was years ago) and pitch
             the bottle
at the trash can. The dog's eyes work the road and his ears straighten at the sound
             of clanking glass.

I lapse back into the sun-baked chair. I wonder about my body, here, in this chair.
What must it look like from the road?
What does the dog think of its smell?
Is this guilt? Could I have been wrong before?

Most of the time I am content with corn dogs and wine
and bumming along from house to house,
a renter, a watcher, never an owner to be,

a loafer who makes as little as possible
so that taxes and contributions are minimal — a vacant plan.

But this work is not the work,
the protest, of Lorca or Neruda,
nor the work of Ginsberg.

In a veil of dust I consider the worth of the silent protest,
of a black dog wagging its tail for no good reason, and what worn
and tempered resistance might wait in the holes
of the trucks stretched together by chicken wire,
what bottles might hold ships,
and what designs might wash up in the bones.

I want to trudge through the dust to the minimart, named the Trading Post,
       a block away.
I want to write a poem for a guy, named Jamie,
who got brained, skull cracked, beaten with a wrench in the parking lot of the
       Dang Bar.

Jamie who was a tough fucker, tough, although not a tough name, Jamie, the guy
who a loud mouth tried to get me to fight one night at a holiday celebration,
just to see who would win. I think the mouth had money on it.

Don't know who he picked or what the odds were. But Jamie and I just shook
hands and drank beer until we tied a heavy canvas army strap around the mouth
and dangled him from a pole, and I remember how clear the half moon shone.

And the moon stayed bright over a single wide trailer as ridiculous tennis shoes
lashed in the air and cigarettes were demanded. But this isn't the poem.
And I can't write a poem for Jamie whose better now, but not the same, slower,
went from the guy who arranges manifests and gives out trucking assignments
at the beer distributor back to the guy who hauls the kegs. The place he began.

All I can do is think of wooden floors, getting to work on time, staying respectable,
and that great forefinger of God that Kerouac sees pointing at him over
      the Rocky Mountains
as Colorado rises from flatlands to peaks, as Jamie wipes at the distant
      January sun

47

that's late to show in a trailer window that's long been done in by cheap shot.
In the winter of the same year I sat in zazen meditation in the house of Mr. Johnson,
a man with swollen knuckles and enormous hands from years of use. The light
low spreading
      a blackish brown
over the walls shelved high in books, the carefully tailored plants in shadow,
I thought of Jamie's skull again. That moment before the crack he must have
      been fierce.
He was fighting two guys, the story goes, and one was sprawled face down in the
      parking lot.
The other squared up in front of him, but with his hands down, his mouth bloodied
      and his eyes
spent, Jamie about ready to let him stay standing and go back in and get a beer,
having made his point, then the skull was suddenly surprised by a splinter in what
      had seemed
to be connected forever and what had been a moment of mercy was now
      fused to a blank
space in the universe where red becomes more texture than color. With the
      hard clap

of wooden blocks, the counting of my breath pops to pause, then gone again
and I bow deeply with my hands closing in on the tile floor, stand and resume
meditation in the vertical plane. That may be last I hear from Jamie.

AND SO THE WAR BEGAN
for Miles Waggener

The Masked Troglodyte,
        the Abyssinian Strangler,
                the Sinister Orangutan and others
whose names have been lost were to wrestle
the night Federico Garcia Lorca was killed,

and wrestle they did while Neruda waited
for his friend to take his seat beside him.

As Troglodyte,
        Strangler,
                and Orangutan flipped,
punched, and pinned the crowd to their excitement,
what face did Neruda wear next to that empty chair?

Where did he learn what sat beside him
that night? Was it another poet
who brought the terrible words?
Was it in the open air of the evening that he overheard
the news? All thoughts are threats,

and so the war began with a poet missing
the matches. Missing those great twists of arms,
shuffling of boots, bantering and boasts,
        those bright masks of life
                competing with Troglodyte, Strangler, and Orangutan.

Tonight I think of poets I've known and cry
for they will come for all of them eventually.

Up from my heart a great shadow steps, bayonet fixed,
its heels heavy and even, it marches to meet some loneliness,
        I'm only now finding.

Tonight they've already made me into a soldier.

TWO DAYS PAST APRIL 5th, 1997

*"...and you there standing before me in the sunset, all your glory in your form!
A perfect beauty of a sunflower!"*
                                                          —Allen Ginsberg

*"I had a dream where Allen Ginsberg went by the name The Ginz and he fixed
small things like phones, radios, refrigerators, Teelp, and the world."*
                                                          — Jaba Jabowski

Still can't think of Allen Ginsberg, The Ginz, while so close to his going
          looms our concept of time as heavy and messy as the mud-snow on
          the surrounding mountains.
I wash at the dishes, clean up the house, dust all over shelves, sort the music,
          alphabetize books on book shelves, clean up and out the desk ...
but stomach still gurgles at regular intervals when I sit. The Ginz is gone in
          body form.
I clean out closets, pitch old worn gloves with rips in the thumbs, socks with
          no matches, boots worn to holes. I do the laundry, dirty up clothes as
          fast as possible so I can do them again.
This of course is what gets done when bodies of the great ones go.
I re-pot plants, get the growers in bigger pots, and write letters about the
          heavy snowfall and nothing much in general to faint relatives and
          friends not seen or heard from in years.
When my grandpa died, when Cactus Ed died, when Shawn Clark died, when
          my cat died, when Bukowski died, when my grandma died, when at
          times I think of Kerouac's death or Lorca's or Wilde's even if they
          were (according to that flawed but popular notion of time) a long
          time ago, the places get clean then at these times.
Bathrooms get scrubbed, rings and leaks on tiles get caulked or limed away
          or scrubbed gone.
So now at this time on April 7, 1997 the house is clean as I can think of, and I
stand at the porch with elbows rested heavy on warped wood and
          stare at the tracks of children's sleds that have worn the snow to the
          rocks.
Nothing left so I think of The Ginz and *economics* and that now nicely I
          won't need postage stamps when I write him. I won't need to count
          on US Post Office or someone else's labors except my own now
          when I keep up my end of the correspondence with The Ginz.

Two Days Past April 5th, 1997

But still thoughts drift off dirty snow and nothing to lick around here, and so

I'll see if the neighbor needs help in the yard I suppose; and alas
what more can I do? what more to do but think of Allen Ginsberg,
so I think of Allen Ginsberg, The Ginz, and I think of Allen
Ginsberg.
And with the dripping water plopping onto the thawing grass I decide the sur-
rounding mountains
can have the mud-snow and decide to let the dust collect itself, a
little, and I think of Allen Ginsberg, The Ginz, Allen Ginsberg.

FRACTURE

Beginning of the work shift. Noon.
Steve, manager, skinny, barely over a 100 pounds,
sixteen or so, my age, lifeguard —
shortly an obvious irony because it's true.

He tells me, "I didn't expect to see you here today,"
as I lean on a counter in a wet office
with a light blue painted floor.
"I just thought…" His eyes drop from mine
to the wet floor cutting him off,
tipping me off I shouldn't be here, but I was waiting
watching out the window
over the pool and the thunderhat clouds
beginning to pile over the Cerbat Mountains —

He went on
         with the obvious
                  "didn't you hear?"

And to this my body reacted.
My body registered light
swim trunks, dark blue,
city pool, white letters,
the total of a uniform;
the sun through the window
warm on my right shoulder and back;
my body ridiculously young, a few scars
there and there, but smooth and easy,
short hair, body hair tanned blonde-invisible. The body made distractions of itself.

Get to it. Get to it.

Steve steps closer as if to place
a hand or hold me,
a body to soothe the words,
but stops at half a step,
eyes pop up to mine
as if nothing is soothed

with the body among men,
more exactly, among boys at age 16, among boys.

         Shawn Clark. Car Wreck. Dead.

On the counter
     I ask a few
         "hows" "whens" "wheres"

*This is the first I've written of Shawn in the past dozen years since. Hard for
me to believe it's been that long.* Shawn Clark, close friend, then of eight
years, died while driving to Golden Valley. Died while driving out of town to
his father's house. Not drunk. Not speeding. Not run off the road by some
unswerving drama. Just driving, then wrecked.

Offered the day off
I countered by counting
the day's crew.
I stayed.
"No point in ruining the rotation."

There have been plenty of the deaths that happen in families, my family, since
then and tears cried in showers or alone with the floor, but not when it's time to
work — plenty of deaths nearer now to me than Shawn Clark's, but his was my
first. I could make him small, but I can't.

At every death I recall I stay, work, hope for work, make work.
What's this do?   *It's a bluff.*

Because I have no faith in time?
I have no faith in time.
That must have been when it started,
     if we can start with no time.
Then, the sun, a blade applied by the day,
       shaved my body smooth,
         and time was something that I clocked in on.
My questions were muted out of a mouth
working below the sunken weight

Fracture

under the balls of the eyes;
the first sign that my body
didn't fit me anymore.

Is time the body?

That day:
I wanted the thunderhat clouds
to be bigger than me, more
of a man in the air than the boy
that I was on the ground.
I wanted lightning. I wanted to leave.
I wanted to blame it on the sky!

I walked to my first stand, my hands gangly, big,
sweat on the fingertips, as if to drown the prints
from the dumbness of themselves.
The toes gripped each step across the hot, white concrete —

For the first time I felt naked
as I walked. I was afraid of it,
but I didn't think of God then
or ever at times of death,
and I believe you're supposed to.

Then, I believed in science and time,
so I worked, although by no means hard work,
compared to the factories that would follow,
but I was clocked in, accounted for.
Lola Fulmer, Roy Fulmer, Jim Jay Sr.
all died and I never missed a day.

When Allen Ginsberg died April 5th, 1997
I had moved faith to words, detested time
and thought of science as mere pieces of a story,
but I still worked when I caught word,
which surprised me because I thought I knew better.

Where was my faith?

When I was eighteen Allen Ginsberg's "Howl" thumped adrenaline, enraged passion: fear/love/horror, which is to say self seeing self.

I had visions!
He spoke with wild hands in my dreams!

I bellowed volumes of his words in dormitory halls, drunk, stumbling and inebriated with image! Drunk with a self that was more than mine.
I stuck his book in my back pocket and hauled it about.
I read on busses in whispers, read around campfires to no one, someone or the air, and that father he was then to me, was in 1997 dead in body form.

So I worked a habit.

Two days later I wrote a poem/elegy that crawled
like a bug from my ear.
I cleaned house, wished I had more work,
and sat in a sparkling better homes and apartment
without feeling clean.

But the real poem for Allen Ginsberg
—who I called The Ginz in long scrawling scroll letters with cutup pictures of Chuck Norris/pop culture, and still he wrote back postcards often times starting with the words
      of Li Po *the birds have vanished down the sky*
      Now the last cloud drains away—
but my real poem for Allen Ginsberg never had his name in it; I wrote it a few days ago; I wrote about his sunflower and my camphorweed — the same in the soul in the soil in the roots.

So maybe I'm ready for Shawn Clark, too distant for tears.

Grief: a chimp under a canopy of leaves
    peering at the mist filtered sun
    that won't admit it's really shining
    from the center of the earth.

Is that right?

Fracture

It leads me back to before:
I'd make fun of my body
if it looked now
like it did when Shawn died.
    I think this has to do with the body,
    an incomplete story.
I'd be too smooth, scarless,
no broken noses, not enough
fat for the cold, soft pretty knuckles.
But do I miss that body that used to fit?

I'm talking mind anyway?
or was it soul?
or is it the same?

But that body of then in the now would mean
I didn't pay, so it would look absurd
in bar light where I continually find me.
And who is paid? Something has happened and it costs. Who? Should I ask what?

Grief/thief/relief: listen.

Can I hear the body
of Shawn Clark then,
or mine then in the now?
What of those bodies
that have been converted to time — the currency of story?

Which is to think of the bones
of Shawn Clark's hands, white scaled, cracked,

which is touch and his surprise
of finding his blood surrounding
his body, his blood separate and working
internally and touched again
on the surface of the skin
in a roof smashed car,
upside down, glass spread
like confetti and movement
in any direction a shard,

another fracture, another cut,
a release of the internal
demanded by the external.

Which might be to say he died alone,
        but he didn't.
He merely died afraid — conscious
filled with foreign context —

left only to conclude
that the flicker of lights
       on boulders
       were the stars falling
       under the suggestion
           of their own weight.

THE CAPTAIN

IN FLAGSTAFF

for Greg Pape

The long sunrise —
the Rio de Flag is full
of snow.

The long sunrise —
on the legs of the cold wind,
my walk.

The long sunrise —
my empty stomach grows satiated
by the smell of pine.

The long sunrise —
gravel and ice disturbed by my boots
wake a fenced dog.

The long sunrise —
my hands open and close
open and close.

The long sunrise —
a street lamp turns off,
then the next one.

The long sunrise —
a car,
the first one.

The long sunrise —
the stalks of the black eyed susans
still stand up!

HIGH IMPERIALISM

The forearm-long dolls being fobbed off as Kachinas wear RW on the heel of the right foot. RW, Roy Wertowski, Junior High Social Studies teacher, retired, Bobcats football coach, retired, a big round man who tools with scraps of wood and canvas and sells the results in county fairs. But he's not in on this scam. Or is he? You tell me. Here's how it goes.

A small Navajo man, (who won't even whisper his own name anymore), his hands broken into hooks over the years, picks the dolls up at the fairs and sells them by his series of hand-painted highway signs that read "Don't Miss the Chief," then "Here's the Chief," then "Stop You've Missed Us," then "Friendly Indians Behind You. Turn Back." From the side of the road and surrounded by these signs, he takes in bills and coins and peels back the change one paper at a time, one coin at a time, saying nothing, and folks pull over to use his out-house, stretch theirs legs, let their dogs run, or eye the tables of trinkets and rugs. Looking for sparks, colors, textures to imitate in his garage, Wertowski one day stops in and spots the RW dolls. He picks one up, rolls it over his big fingers and palm. He likes it. Something about the light out there, perhaps, the red dust over the plywood table, or the rez dogs and coyotes just over the brush eyeing the collared poodles, or maybe he just doesn't want any trouble, so he likes the dolls there, and at the next county fair he simply doubles his prices, they both nod on it, and the man with the hooked hands doubles his prices.

So is Roy Wertowski in on it? What about the man with the hooked hands? Well, I don't know. I can tell you this. I stopped by his place on the side of the road for a stretch, got out, walked, saw the shitting poodles, the folks in line for the outhouse, a handful of people combing the blankets and necklaces, saw the dolls, swore the last *official* sign I saw read "Navajo Nation," and I closed in on what looked like shards of a Barbie wardrobe over balsa, pine, and ironwood stuck together under a veil of tan, white, and black paints. Flipping the dolls, tugging the capes, lifting the cloth, I spotted my fingers being watched by the man while his hooks finished slowly making change for the customer in front of him. I extended the doll, began to speak, but on my arm he placed his hand, surprisingly gentle for such a man-gled thing, and I could hear a laugh, maybe just a breath, barely audible in the dry air, and he gave me the doll for nothing. Now, I don't know if I'm in on it, but at home I keep the doll on a prominent shelf and from such a height hear stories.

A LOVE STORY

My cactus died yesterday.
I watered it,
     watered it,
          watered it,
               watered it,

but

     it just wilted
like an over-sized raisin, green.

I wanted to know the problem,
so I yanked it from its marshy pot.

The needles drove into my hand,
and my fresh blood mixed

with the stale phlegm
that dropped from its core.

A buddy of mine, Thor,
suggested that I over-watered.

I shrugged my deaf shoulders
and washed my dirty and indifferent hands.

Today, I bought a new cactus,
rushed home, and planted it in my toilet.

ON 6th STREET
for Ophelia Doom

The ravens perch on the limbs of the elms in the park outside my window. I sip warm coffee, slowly, and a man in chain mail armor, who wears a long, dirt-red cape that dangles from his back and crumples into the grass, sits straight on a weathered park bench. His right arm props up a grey shield. A broad sword dangles from his hand; its metal weight rests against his left leg. He looks at the traffic moving in puffs up Sixth Street on this February afternoon. I sip my coffee, turn my attention to the grey sky hovered over the elms, hovered over the ravens. All summer and fall in the park, men dressed like knights arrived on Sundays. I watched through the dirty glass of my window. Today, this one looks to be the only show. I finish the rest of my coffee, fiddle with the newspaper in front of me, thumb through "Sports," thumb through "World Events" quickly. The ravens still perch, the sky still lingers over the elms, the knight still sits straight. I consider putting on my heavy jacket and joining him. I regard him like a man who owes debts. With no knight gear to speak of, I can offer him only an ordinary wrestling match in the brown grass, something to keep the ravens happy. I jostle through the paper, past the "classifieds" and set it on the table. I consider the ravens and the traffic and the sky. I stand and turn to the kitchen with my mug in hand and wait for the leaves to sprout from the limbs of the elms.

ON SHAKESPEARE
for Todd Gentry

Histories: these guys needed
        some money,
so they rolled
        some guys.
Turned out to be
        the wrong guys.

Comedies: this girl
        thought she could
get some things off these guys,
        wrong guys.

Romances: this girl
        fell in love with some guys.
Turned out to be
        the wrong guys.

Tragedies: this guy
        wanted to be
a big time guy,
        wrong guy.

JUNE

The awful silliness of sprinklers
spit spit spit spit.

MORNING AT THE DESERT INN MOTEL

In the space between
the door and the frame the songs
of the birds come in —

PHILOSOPHY

I-80   70MPH
        I look off the road
             a huge, huge

             rainbow ring
        around the sun.
Why?

Don't know.

A huge, huge
        rainbow ring
             around the sun.

MILES OF DIRT TO COVER
for Ron French

He tailed us for hours through the summer heat of long, straight Texas roads. And you, who I'd known only a year, drove while my mother sat quiet in the front seat and my brother and I made small shifts to look behind. You sped up our car, slowed us down, pulled over once, but the man pulled off behind us and waited. You pulled back on the road. Sped up. What else was there to do? The man swerved out after us and followed so close that from our back seat I could sneak glances of his face drenched in sweat, the straight edges of his cheeks, the dirty brown layers of coat, on flannel, on T-shirt, his large hands gripping the wheel.

You whipped us over again, quicker. The man, forced to pull over in front, waited about forty yards ahead. I don't remember seeing how you got there, but you were half way to his car and walked in long strides with your .357 held straight down on your right side. You closed. I propped my head over the front seat and squinted. The man sat still. You stopped just behind his door. I could not hear what was said, but it was just a few seconds, then you let him go.

A few hours down the road we stopped at a two story motel, and I laid awake in bed beside my brother; our bodies still small enough to fit in a single. Under thin sheets I wished you had shot the man. I imagined the car head-lights peering through the dark, you tracking him all night, catching up to him at day break in a truck stop diner. I could see your arm raised and your revolver pointing as straight as the horizon shining into his numb face. I want-ed to know that man's head had been leveled, clean from his shoulders, blown apart and the pieces a mess of nothing. I didn't want it to be like a movie where the good guy lets the bad guy go with a warning, until the bad guy blows it again, and the white hat has to be put back on and miles of dirt cov-ered before the last show down. I wanted to fast forward to the scene where the boy, who fetches water and ropes and other small but useful things, thanks the hero, comes up with the right line or two to say, the well-timed tear, the sun light pin-pointing the grass, the magic that glues it all together, but this was no film where we stew and spin above miranda days. I had no words, right ones or wrong, but you stayed anyway and knew what to level and what not to level and I say thank you, late.

TO RUINS ON THE MOGOLLON RIM

for Doris Potokar

The cattle are colored
       like your bleached stones
              broken by brown splotches

of juniper. I identify
       their familiarity first
              at the top of this mesa. Then

I find myself amazed
       at your closeness
              to the interstate,

so near
       that engines
              and jake brakes

are as much background
       as the wind.
              What sounds

you have stood through!
       Was this a part
              of your plan, your design?

I guess your design
       Sinagua.
              The state park

to the south designates
       those ruins as such
              and pictographs to the north

have been mapped
       as the same —
              so my guess

is made by theirs,
       but what's yours?

JOURNEYMAN

He dreamed he woke in the middle of the night no more certain that his body was his than he was certain his words were. The night rolled to him in waves, waves falling silently, exhausted before a rock laden coast. The salty mist he tasted as green apples, then the pass of their gentle acid from the tongue. He pulled his arm across his chest and light swirled with its shadows. The biceps in tight contraction couldn't stand up to the shadows and cramped, fatigued, and only trusted the fingers for meaning. The fingers frightened into fascination brushed the arm, and the brush was like language babbled by a child, language that makes grown ups laugh and smile, then take another sip from their empty glasses, the comfort quickly forgotten in the show of lights. If this man could be taken up now by a mountain, he would. He would be swept above the rocks of the coast with his body packing nothing but the bruises of language.

The sweat on the brow
a morning mist watering —
fuel by noon.

MY FAILED PLANS

Write a poem
        each day.
Don't spend all my money
        at the bar.
Do 100 push ups
        each day.
Do 100 sit ups
        each day.
Lose fat
        off my gut.
Sleep
        with that sexy bartender.
Keep up
        on my correspondence.

Well, this isn't much
        of a poem, but
I suppose, today, I did one thing
        on my list.

I sure as hell aint dropping
to give you some reps,
and that bartender is serving
dirty looks for nothing
        all night.

A SLOW TRAIN TO MID-MORNING

The sign outside the train window reads "Yago Café" in bold, block,
red letters pressed into a yellow painted, plywood placard
as big as a car. From your seat, your eyes whittle away the traffic,
and the train continues to stay. The French bread in hand remains stale.

The sign outside the train window reads "Yago Café." The dust collects
slowly on your jeans, on the shoulders of your shirt, on the top of your head.
The Yago Café lingers on a wall on Main Street in the center
of America, which is the center of the world, which is the center

of the universe. Of course, you know that and you don't even need
to ride to the Yago Café to know. You don't even need to read or write
or paint or scrawl. You don't even need your crayons to know the Yago
Café sign is the center. It's obvious with simple math and straight reasoning.

It's as obvious as the fact that the bell hop won't be by or the conductor's
not coming to check your forged ticket. You know it the way you know the bread
isn't fresh. The Yago Café - you recognize the red, you recognize the yellow,
you recognize the monstrous plywood. You know the train isn't going

to start rolling again because there's no place to go other than the center.
And so your reason concludes there won't be lunch, logical, not even
a left-over daily soup; you've missed breakfast and nobody in America eats
brunch anymore, and that's hard to take seriously, at least from your seat, so don't.

The sign outside the train window reads "Yago Café" in bold, block,
red letters pressed into a yellow painted, plywood placard as big as a car. The sign inside
the window reads "Yago Café," and the window has "Yago Café" scribbled all over it
in the small splattered guts of flies and bugs and dirts streaked by no rains.

MCDONALD'S UPSOLD

Two children race through the smell of grease,
into the counter bang their extended arms: the most basic of brakes.

One leaps up down until winded, eyes stuck
the entire time to the McTeenager on the register,

the long, lanky McTeen who runs the show,
who keeps the McEverything flying over the counter!

The children ask for the radio to be changed
to N'Sync. The Mc explains it's MUZAC

and he can't do anything
about it. The leaping stops.

"What's MUZAC?"
            "It's a tape."
"What's on it?"
            Heavy gulps of breathing fill the silence.

Where are the parents?
Where is the next customer? Where's the backup?
More air is exchanged, hopping resumes.

"No, really, what's on it?"
            they croon
            "what's on it?"
                        What's on it:
the sweetest song
on any station.

CAPTAIN ROWE

Captain Rowe was like a fist. His bald head wide and continually stern, his neck and shoulders slabs of meat, barrel chested, a shade under six feet tall, he made his way through the world with heavy heel toe steps.

Currently, the United States Army assigned Captain Rowe to Kentucky to work on computers, his thick fingers writing program one day after the next. He'd been in fourteen years and was looking for one of the early retirement routes, just needed to work the numbers out. He'd been promised early retirement for years, then they ran out of those slots, then he could have a prorated deal, then... and then they went on and on. Whatever drew Captain Rowe to the Army had long since died. It got him through school, got him out of the country for a while, moved him around enough so that great, lonely air in the middle of even the tightest fist never had time to think about what it didn't get to touch.

He used theater to map where he'd been in his Army career. Shakespeare was his primary marker, although he'd see the occasional Marlowe play and had caught a Ben Johnson Festival in Eugene, Oregon. His years in Flagstaff, Arizona were highlighted by the University's three plays per year. Always the staple of *Romeo and Juliet* and *A Midsummer Night's Dream*, but the repetition never bothered him. The students were sincere, hardworking, if not convincing. Flagstaff also had a small independent theater, Theatrikos, which was irregular but surprising with its performances. In diners alone, he recalled the excellent acoustics of its 100 chair auditorium. Butte, Montana helped him with its Irish Everlast Theater Company switching from the staple of plays by Yeats, Wilde, Beckett, and doing *King Lear* for two weeks in February when the temperature never rose above zero. Spokane, Washington was the worst; Postmodern confusion was the only thing stirring in the University and no local action. The low budget, in the park, single scene efforts of Smith, South Dakota charmed him. Thin voiced men shouting soliloquies to the trees, water paint backdrops falling on top of unfazed actors, the cardboard sword bending at all the wrong times. In Kentucky Captain Rowe fed himself on a staple of BBC videos from the library and hoped for the best. He knew it wouldn't be enough.

Flagstaff, Arizona and the calling of what might be showing may have drove him AWOL as much as anything else, that drama down the road, hard to say about these things. What breaks a man? Can a man only be broken when he wants to be? Captain Rowe packed his GMC with ten evenly sized boxes; eight of which contained his video collection, one more for CDs and cassettes, one for books; with him in the cab he kept his laptop, boom box, television,

VCR player (he never bothered investing in DVD - he knew the trend wouldn't last as long as 8 track). The truck packed, he finished the last two beers in the refrigerator, then spread a gallon of gasoline throughout his one bedroom apartment located in the packed dirt lot behind the Catholic Church. The smell of fumes followed him out the doorway. A pitch of a match and up it went, and out of Kentucky the Captain drove, heading to your town.

CAMPHORWEED

SHIT CITY

As a Marxist I've washed dishes and windows; been a janitor who can vanish
into a mop bucket, scrubbed my will to resist clean and shiny as a
commercial.

As a Marxist I've sold shoes to the poor, the poor middle class, and the
bourgeois alike, all looking for a deal. Continually discounted, an
amalgamation of corporate punches to the register, and we're good
to go. Buy one, get half off the next you don't need.
Buy one, I'll give you the other. Buy one. Buy one. Buy one.

As a Marxist I've lumped furniture: presswood fall apart shelves; eternally
nicked dressers; warped and unassembled bed rails from the God of
Misfits and Bent Bolts; Persian rugs, the light side always facing the
wrong way; high boys, file cabinets, fire safes, gun racks; you name
it, I'll lump it from Shit City, USA to Shit City, Wherever.

As a Marxist I've worked shipping docks where the same shit takes a ride on
the incessantly swallowing sea.

As a Marxist I've delivered pizzas and dope, burned out clutches doing both.

As a Marxist I've reground plastics, dumped polysomethingoranother slag
into whatever container had room, broke OSHA codes I didn't even
know.

As a Marxist I've hung drywall, trusses, pounded nails, busted every one of
my fingers, my nose, knuckles in Labor's name, amen.

As a Marxist I've been a grounds worker, groundskeeper, dirt digging dolt,
planting exotics I hope will die soon.

As a Marxist I've worked as a monkey wrencher, a vandal whose particulars
I'm too paranoid to divulge even to you.

As a Marxist I've been a hiking guide, tourist guide pointing out the Cairns of
Industrial Tourism, the Markers of High Imperialism on the topo
maps of Exploitation – come take a look!

As a Marxist I've been a lifeguard; I've been a pool cleaner who didn't do
much except get wet and watch pretty girls bikini wrapped in the
ease of summer, while Tibet gets less andless free, while I apply sun
block and soak in the indifferent sun.

As a Marxist I've written copy, proofread, freelanced as a journalist covering
news no one wants to be informed about.

As a Marxist I've been an editor, a publisher of literature no one reads.

As a Marxist I've been a bouncer, a bartender, a waiter who serves drinks I'd
much rather have down my division of labor gulping throat.

As a Marxist I've been a manager of retail, service industry accountant,
bookkeeper, payroll counter, done data entry until every null set gets
bored and adds up to something.

As a Marxist I've been a thief, embezzler. What have you got for me?
As a Marxist I've been a Book Salesman, a Remainder Buyer: a booming
business since the 80s, gouging literature thanks to Reagan and his
tax and spend conservatism. Reagan, the pyro who burned the
Library of Alexandria and my Marxist ass sold the ashes.
Are we all forgiven yet?
As a Marxist I've been a hired crewhand on a yacht filled with the rich and
knotted line and rigging I don't get.
As a Marxist I've been a bodybuilder, a nude model, a Muse for someone's
B-rate chunk of art.
As a Marxist I've worked for the Feds on Fire Control, ran hose off an
engine, flanked beautiful flames, mopped up messes in half a dozen
fuel types, and crawled on my hands and knees to rid the land of
heat.
As a Marxist I've been a wildlife observer, field specialist who counts big
horn sheep until everyone sleeps.
As a Marxist I've been on unemployment. Where's my forms?
As a Marxist I've taught college courses on Marxism under the guide of
Introduction to Poetry and Freshman Comp for who would hire a
Marxist such as me for the likes of such a job?

ANDRE CONTINUES UNDEFEATED STREAK
AT THE AMBOY SPORTS ARENA

And one night Andre the Giant just went up.
Helluva a move really.
Bruiser had had him by the throat,
        white, scarred, fingers clawing and shaking,
                pinching into an upset.
Then, Andre countered by countering gravity.
Andre hefted his great head back,
exhaled and there he went.

It caught on too. Spread like hose water
        through a manicured lawn.
Bruiser and referee drifted
        into the stumped air.
Ring posts with a creek came off.
Ropes, matt, springs, 2" x 4"s, folding chairs washed
        about in an eddy.
The light from the overheads warped
        like Slinkies on stairs.
Pops and clicks of cameras.
Shrieks and clapping of hands.
Some fans spooked, a pack of Wile E. Coyotes whirling in place.
Some searched their programs for a clue.
Bruiser clung to the rafters and cried.
The ref called the whole thing a draw.
The promoter tried to charge for seating
        on the ceiling.
Those in the cheap seats found as good a view as any.
And I was glad to be there,

to see light roam as free as smoke,
to feel the sweat on my face crawl into the clamor,
to smell the joy of bones and muscles
        searching for new functions,
and I was glad to be there, to see what
Andre could really do if pressed,
to see the beauty of humans
        left to feel like angels,
to see myself lost
        in a dome of possibilities,

for the next day the newspapers chalked the whole thing up
    as Sports Entertainment,
and Bruiser, rebuilt by his same old, tough-guy words,
    demanded a rematch at your place.

FRICTION

Sometimes your eyes have enough.
The lights off. You lay in bed in a strange room.

Rub your eyelids — done for the day
your eyes content, then black is all

you feel.
>   No more rabbits plowed into your car.
>   No more employees croon for one more chance
>   before you give them the axe.
>   No more mothers pinch their children
>   on the back of the arms and you keep
>   silent about the whole thing.
Like boys on prom dates, scientists cling to thin, makeup covered theories,
>   corpus callosum and smarts, higher functions, but today
>   you're done being a monster:
retired your claws, the savagery of your eyes hides.

Rub away at 'em. The language of grants and welfare scientists
won't save anything anymore.

They're full of shit.
They'll sell you anything. They just want in your pants.

Outside it's five below zero. This room
may as well be set on Mars. Go outside and you won't make it.

Intelligence holes up in the back,
I mean very back, of your eyes.
You're massaging it right now.
Press harder. It's there.

FLOWER

"...and you there standing before me in the sunset, all your glory in your form!
A perfect beauty of a sunflower!"

—Allen Ginsberg

Camphorweed, brown, dry
on a dead road is still in
the sunflower family.

August winds blowing
its stalk arid and stiff, frail
green evaporating —

yellow flower, small,
withering, darker, darker,
closer to topple —

it still insists sunflower:
the sunflower that first drives
thin roots, an inverted crown,

to the source of the soul
that lives in dead roads.

BRACKEN BRUSH

A flat run of sand, former rock, trickles hot
through my fingers. Miles, long-time wanderer
and tooler around, tells me stories of the past two years:
two years teaching here on the Res.

Atop the cliffs the sand lightly holds the bracken brush, and cliffs of ever falling dust
brush the horizon: a shagged truth. The rock for now
holds its own, and the Navajo Res
seems only a name as the sands in every direction
hold no other humans, no counted years.

Our voices stew and twine with brush,
sands, and cliffs. Senses, the heat of years,
top the edges of speech while today tilts and rocks
the ebbs and flows of reason.

Sitting, Miles rants with arms, and wind,
reservations withheld, chimes in.
The debate: teaching on the Res,
a job... no Romance left... rounded

off views of a writer making a year's
wage... a way to live, groups brushed
together and chiseled into categories, rocks
pounded into names and dates, places, years

summed into smooth abstractions, years
of education ignored by a name like Reservation,
a name and with a heave in the sand I flop,
pitch a rock at the rocks and watch the years of abstraction
fall forward. Miles brushes against the sky, the Res a thought.

SOME POWER

I.

Growing up, the most powerful thing on t.v.
        was Andre the Giant tossing
two or three wrestlers who wouldn't follow the rules,
        crashing them to the matt in flips
and flops, stacking and pinning all three at once
        under his spread hand, big as a chest.
When did Andre the Giant realize
        how big he would be?
"As a teenager," claimed Andre's father,
        "we no longer knew
how strong he was, for there was nothing on the farm
        in Grenoble he could not lift."
What would it be like to be so big
        that fists were a moot point?
To even the cruelest, you could extend
        your hand without fear.

II.

My mother, when I was a boy, was held up,
        tied at gunpoint at the grocery store
where she worked. She pulled the ropes
        hard enough to knock over
the nearby phone, and the box boy
        dialed the police with his tongue.
Since she made minimum and my brother and I
        needed food, the next day
she opened the store, ringing into the register
        with strong fingers, without pause.
I'd hope some of the strength
        of her hands rubbed into mine,

for tonight I sit in a chair, alone, with my heart
        beating at nearly 200 beats per minute.
(I know because I timed it.)
        A constant pounding of my heart
not to take the shape of a fist,
        not to take hold of headlines:

Some Power

Anthrax in Nevada, New York, etc.
Contaminated Package Sent to Tom Brokaw
Ground Troops Deployed
Uzbekistan a Surprising Ally

The muscles of my fingers cramp:
        hooks.
So much scar tissue and hate, calluses.
        Tonight I'd enlist in any army.

III.

By the time I was eighteen there was nothing
        on a football field I couldn't hit harder than.
Almost nothing on a matt I couldn't stick.
I roamed parties in the desert looking
        for the stray story by thieves
by bonfire and the slip tale
        of robbing a grocery store years ago.

Off I run, the narrative and a flick and spark from his lighter
        revealing his crooked nose
as he lights his cigarette and stares off
        into the night framed mesa.
Then, his accomplice shaded off his shoulder,
        then the next one, then…

This night: feral and full of hate
        and hurt, where does it find the patience
            of a giant? Of a mother?
To know whatever the pounding,
        the heart can hold its own?

CAMPHORWEED

A harris hawk awaits me on a limb
of juniper at eye level. I walk around
the patches of camphorweed as if their stems
were cairns marking places lives got lucky:
the last canteen was enough, the rattlesnake's
venom was dull and didn't kill, that second
shot to die on terms you claim your own,
perhaps resolved.

               Perhaps resolve alone
is fuel enough to raise these seeds to stems
on mining roads abandoned by gold and scattered
with trespass warnings blown face down.
How else to explain why camphorweed
is first in staking out the broken roads?

How else?   My boots stumble, and then I'm struck
with stillness. Looking down these last few steps
has moved my body within arm's stretch of the hawk
I'd forgotten on the juniper, my first attraction.
It stares square at my shoulder, head angled
down like a question mark. I look into
the feathers of its barrel chest in awe of chances
running me so close, the luck of playing
a hawk's game of chicken intent enough
on feet to avoid blinking.

              What chances brought
this hawk to hold this limb I have no idea.
Where there's one harris hawk there's three,
but who's outflanking who out here? Content
to wait for camphorweed to grow around my bones
I circle up my luck as if it were sense.

The hawk's stare and stillness give a flicker
ray approval, but my feet vanish and crack
into caliche, and what I called my body is desert
air, my eyes a mirage left on rocks:
a water's offering to the sky —

THE MAGICIAN
for Ian Rabb

It's been a search filled
with lactic acid, a busted ankle,
hill upon hill on Mogollon Rim
where I can't ascend to the next
with enough speed to see
if he's there or not —

It's become a contest
of pain, mine versus his.
His? His being the pain of having
once been the king of the world
of the Mogollon Rim, which
was, of course, the world whole.

Mine? Harder
to say. There's a hill thick
with prickly pear, thick with hope
on a steep, angled slope rising
to rock, vertical and off
again I go —

LA QUERENCIA

LA QUERENCIA:
MANIFESTO OF THE UNITED STATES
DEPARTMENT OF POETRY

When Daisy Zamora fought as a Sandinista revolutionary in the Nicaraguan Civil War she carried her poems onto the battlefield. She says she couldn't have survived without them. Jimmy Santiago Baca was berated, spit upon, beaten, and put his life in danger when, while incarcerated, he decided to read and keep with him a book, rather than his title as gang leader. Baca's faith stayed with the words in the book because he knew it had answers to his questions, and he knew it would ultimately save his life. Poetry has always served as a talisman against evil, against the mundane, against the doldrums, against tyranny—including all the monstrosities of petty tyranny, which Ed Abbey claims is the worse kind of tyranny. Petty tyranny dehumanizes, and its deceptively diminutive stature leaves nothing noble for its victim to resist.

Despite presidential war drums and doom and gloom newspaper headlines, for most Americans the real tyranny in the United States is mainly of the sort Ed Abbey identifies, petty tyranny. This is not to say there isn't a real threat out there. Corporate America's atrocities against the land, the endless miles of clear-cuts, the rivers so polluted that they catch fire, the casual pollution of the air, the rigid class system held secure by the watered down racism of the media, all blend into the back of the mind and mask themselves as an abstraction. The numbers are too big to crunch. The sensations too vague and overwhelming. The threat too removed. These monstrosities are not the Spanish conquistadors hacking Aztecs in half with swords for sport, daily rapes of natives as regular as morning breakfast, the slavery and annihilation of whole cultures; or moving closer to our past, these are not the U.S. government's genocide policy and extermination of Native American tribes. These tyrants engaged in what would now be vivid and detectable slaughters that we would vehemently protest, if happening now in the exact same form and frequency. Hitler, for example, was a half century or so past the time when genocide was acceptable. He also practiced his monstrous policies on people in Europe and, probably most importantly, seemed like a genuine threat to us, so we put on a righteous garb and moral superiority and took him to task. Rightfully so. This, of course, was needed and admirable and many of those who took part in the battle, both on the field and back home, knew what they fought against was wrong and that their resistance and sacrifice for a better good was worth it.

But the threat there was immediate and tangible, with the Corporate America threat we have nothing tangible to fight against, and we're already outflanked by the petty anyway. One fight at a time, fellas. Our random rages and outbursts in the face of honking rush-hour traffic, tele-marketers, defective merchandise, and paperwork circles to nowhere, addictions to drugs, food, gambling and so on make no sense to us. We are baffled—*I was sane and happy a minute ago, why am I full of rage or despair now?* Psychologists continually note increasing mental illness in all levels of our society and may do the best they can, but, at best, they are only medics treating an endless stream of victims.

How can we fight against tyranny when Corporate America has removed the ground right from under us? We are like Antaeus off his feet and hoisted in the air by a Herculean Monster; we feel weak and think we are getting weaker with no way of imagining how to get down from the strangling iron grip around our body. In addition to fierce strength, the monster bellows forth savagely powerful rhetoric. It tells us the sky is where we belong, fills us with so much gibberish that we don't even know what's in store and what potential we have, if we can only get a desperate toe to the earth.

The strategies for rejuvenation and existence though are not the same as previous type battles with Conquistador Nightmares, U.S. Indian Bounty Hunter Plagues, or Hitler Storm Trooper Mechanized Death Drones. The Corporate enemy is very different, so the fight is very different. Corporate America has the power and is using it at a faster and faster pace to potentially destroy not just human life and human ecosystems, but in its hunger and greed and arrogance, to destroy virtually all life, leaving only insects, bacteria, and viruses (which are all much tougher than Corporate America). The threat to life is absolute, yet the weapons are veiled in abstraction, and being "informed" about current events merely points us in the wrong direction.

It is for the above reasons that I'm eternally an optimist. The petty tyrannies screw with our heads, hearts, souls. This is where the battlefields sits now. They're fighting on our own ground, and we certainly know the territory better—even if they think that advertising has out-scouted us here as well. They're wrong. We should fight on our turf. Not theirs. We won't confuse the map with the territory anymore.

The Spanish word *la querencia* refers to a place in a bullring where the wounded bull goes to gather himself, to regroup. Barry Lopez in *The Rediscovery of*

North America rescues this word from this nasty Spanish context and proposes that *la querencia* is a place where we can go to gather ourselves, to regroup, to become grounded and figure out who we are, and what we might do in the face of a grave challenge. Lopez marries the root of the word, *querer*—to desire, to the connotation of a challenge, possibly a nearly overwhelming challenge, and makes *la querencia* a place of hope in loss. So where do we find our *la querencia*? Where's our ground, our earth?

For me it rests in words, in stories, in poetry, with language and communication. It always has since I can remember, and this is where I attempt to resist, to hold onto whatever makes me human, happy. To this I propose we start The United States Department of Poetry. In fact it's already begun! Unlike boxing, we need no bribe-riddled sanctioning body to give us this title. Unlike government decreed poet laureates, we need no president or governor to grant us titles. (Which they can try to take away when we don't write the poems they want, as in the very recent case of the New Jersey governor who has attempted to remove renowned, New Jersey Poet Laureate, Amiri Baraka, from his position for writing a poem, "Somebody Blew Up America," railing against terrorism and fascism).

The primary vehicle of compassion is seeing, observing, realizing that there is more in the universe than oneself. The ability to communicate with other humans, sentient beings, the natural world, the urban world, and to exist, to observe, and to respond to the multiple, rich surroundings the universe offers us are paramount in leading peaceful, happy lives. I wonder how many poems the New Jersey governor has read? Or if he even read Baraka's poem? Aren't we, as Americans, interested in compassion, quality of life, promoting freedom? Poetry is the vehicle by which the United States Department of Poetry hopes to engage those in the universe. It is our goal to bring to the people poetry that is dynamic and alive. Poetry that reminds us of our own breath, our own worth and the worth of others. Joyful people, overfilled with life and compassion, do not engage in tyranny: colonialism, economic imperialism, petty tyranny, or any other kind of oppression. A land filled with free thinking, compassionate people would simply starve the beast right out of existence. No one gets hurt. CEO's don't want to be the way they are anyway. Now they could put on their nice suits and get jobs as bell hops where they smile all day and get in some good, healthy exercise.

To freedom, I offer some of the Tenets of the United States Department of Poetry: (Of course, you may, and should, add or delete as necessary, and we don't need a majority, a quorum, or electoral college to make those changes. As in any Democracy, we're all in charge.)

I. We memorize poems. We hold poems in our heads and bodies for pleasure and in case of emergency. Preparedness is paramount. When you find yourself dull and waiting in the line at the bank or supermarket. When you find yourself driving a flatbed of pallets to the chipper for yet another day. When you find yourself surrounded by a cubicle one Monday after the next. When you find yourself almost ready to push the "ON" button on your remote control. At these times protect yourself! Bring out your poem. Recite your poem. Put yourself in that place and do as you please. Always be armed with poetry.

II. We prize poems that are true. Truth in a Western empirical sense is a child's notion for amateurs. Disregard that idea of truth. Your bones know what is true. Your body knows what is true. When something rings true, you feel it in your guts, in your heart. Your brain is the last to catch on. When has your brain ever been in charge of anything important? We seek to read or to write poems that ring true to the body and the mind.

III. Be generous with poetry. Poetry is our primary means of compassion, share it. Get involved with everything you possibly can, then get involved with a little more. If you're a teacher of poetry, then volunteer to teach at prisons, at adult education classes, in elementary schools, and so on. If you're new poet, then share your findings, recite poems to friends, mail them to strangers, spread the word. Poetry is magic. Words are magic. Words and the imagery and physical responses they produce are magic. This has been known for a long time.

IV. Do more than you talk about doing. Poetry and compassion are more than coffee circle chats. They are not distant or intellectual. They are in your body. In general, it's better to read a poem than to interpret a poem. This is not to say that some discussion with others excited about poetry is bad. But don't get too smart on yourself, too removed from the source. Always keep the poem close.

Language is a physical act. To read a poem of Dylan Thomas aloud is to breathe, to some extent, in the same manner as Thomas, to explore the same movement of mouth and tongue. The ear gets involved, the eyes, the mouth, the diaphragm, the hands that hold the poem. Poetry is an act of language that

94

prizes the entire body, rewards the mind and the soul. Poems are fighters, and they are made by people who are fighters, wounded, beaten down, but by no means defeated, and in fact may be growing stronger while they figure the ground and measure their next maneuver. With Allen Ginsberg's *Howl* in the back-pocket you're less alone and more sturdy in the face of work that needs to be done. With a Bukowski poem in the brain you can't be taken alone to jail, or abandoned in a no end retail job, or stuck with any number of shit jobs. The best poems both work in protest against something and propose an alternative.

Poems are our Antaeus' dirt, our *la querencia*, an alternative to trotting about with open wounds and burning lungs. After being hoisted up for so long and told that this is where we want to be, the return to the ground becomes complicated. These poems know the way down. In them we find both a place to go for rest and a breath and a place to feel big again, to feel an inkling of humanity, which with some luck may spark into a plan for existence and a vibrant dynamic life within the jaws of the beast.

Like our patriotic hero, John Hancock, I cannot sign this paper boldly enough. Please sign your name alongside the rest of us.

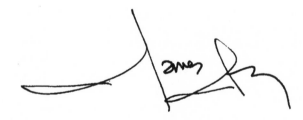

Poetry is a weapon loaded with the future.
—Gabriel Celaya; trans: Miles Waggener

NOTES

"And So the War Began": The story of Pablo Neruda waiting for Garcia Lorca the night of his friend's execution was sent to me by the American Poet, Miles Waggener, and immediately I began writing down my own response to this history. I spent quite a bit of time researching the particulars of Spanish professional wrestling during that era and concluded finally that this didn't matter for purposes of the poem. I envisioned the professional wrestling I have seen from this era and the poets I have known from this time and transposed them into the history. So if you're looking for an accurate description of wrestling in Granada during the Civil War, then do not look to this poem. And especially do not look to history books.

"Andy Devine": Andy Devine is best known for his role as Jingles in numerous Westerns. A room dedicated to his film career is located at the Dam Bar in Kingman, Arizona.

"A Boy's Knuckles Swollen": The epigram is taken from an interview in *Rasslin' Now* with Jack Hutchinson, two-time cruiserweight champion.

"Flower": The epigram is from Allen Ginsberg's poem, "Sunflower Sutra," *Howl and Other Poems.*

"Bedingfield": CCC stands for the Civilian Conservation Corps, established in 1933 as part of President Roosevelt's New Deal program. FDR created the CCC partly for conservation of the country's natural resources and mainly to provide work for unemployed men during the Depression.

"Fracture": The Li Po lines are from the poem, "Zazen on the Mountain."

"High Imperialism": University of Montana Professor, Bob Baker, inspired the title, through his lecture on the British Period of High Imperialism. While listening to his lecture, the onslaught of Industrial Tourism in the Southwest came to my mind. Read Edward Abbey's *Desert Solitaire* for more on Industrial Tourism.
"In Flagstaff": The form of the poem is inspired by Japanese haiku master, Buson.

"S.S. Dorchester": The S.S. Dorchester was the ship on which Jack Kerouac served while in the Merchant Marines during WWII. It was sunk by a German U-boat three months after Kerouac left the Merchant Marines. All hands were lost.

"The Magician": The story of the Magician, a Sinagua Chief, was told to me by Greg Pape and further elucidated by Arnold Johnson.